Jack the Ripper

ILLUSTRATED

CALIBER
COMICS

WRITER
GARY REED

ARTIST
MARK BLOODWORTH

LETTERER
CHET JACQUES

EDITOR
JAMES PRUETT

COVER ART
MARK BLOODWORTH

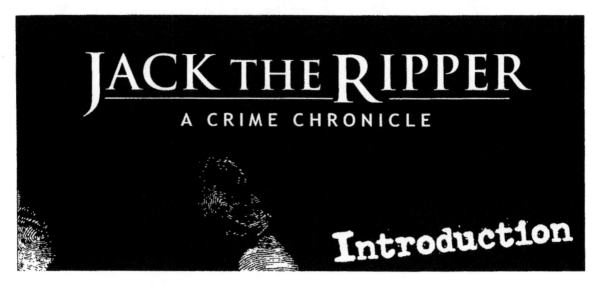

JACK THE RIPPER
A CRIME CHRONICLE

Introduction

The story of Jack the Ripper is certainly not a complete one. For over 100 years, the mystery of Jack the Ripper has thrilled and enthralled countless investigators, both professional and amateur. Possibly, only the assassination of John F. Kennedy has brought up more intrigue and debate.

There is a considerable amount of information on Jack the Ripper, but the final clues as to his true identity are yet be had. Even with intensive research and extrapolation of incredible detail, we still don't know who Jack the Ripper was or even a consensus on who are the leading suspects. In fact, it's not even clarified how many victims there were.

This issue of Crime Chronicles is not meant to be an exhaustively researched expose on Jack the Ripper, nor will any one theory be proposed. It is, rather, a general survey of the field of Ripperology. It will present the basic facts that are known, cover the most viable theories, and attempt to provide enough information to allow a curious reader a rudimentary understanding of the Ripper Legacy. If this overview intrigues you into learning more about the Ripper, there is an incredible amount of material that delves deep into the lives of the victims, the investigation of the crimes, and of course, the many theories of who was Jack the Ripper. Some of the books out there are excellent, whereas others tend to take facts and stretch incredible theories from a seed of reality. But that's a great part of the "fun" in dealing with Jack the Ripper...the exploration of the theories and guesses. Of course, some may be upset that people "enjoy" the research aspects of Jack the Ripper as the crimes were real and they were brutal. But the fans of Ripperology understand that and in no way does the enjoyment aspect cloud the terrible fates that the victims suffered.

In recent years there has been more information revealed about the Jack the Ripper case and researchers are fairly sophisticated in compiling existing data and building new foundations. For example, the common knowledge of there being five victims of the Ripper is in serious question. There is a general debate on whether one of the established victims actually fell to the knife of the Ripper, and there are others who proposed that other victims, not usually associated with Jack the Ripper, may indeed, be victims of the notorious killer.

One of the obvious questions that is asked is why is Jack the Ripper so famous...or infamous. After all, only five deaths are usually attributed to him. That is hardly a number to strike terror and fear into a world that has seen serial killers that number their victims by the dozens. It wasn't because Jack the Ripper was the first serial killer either, because he wasn't. Some have claimed that his were the first sexual murders but a great deal of that speculation depends on definitions of what a sexual murderer is. The killings were brutal, yes, but there are other examples of terrible murders. So, what was it that made Jack the Ripper different...such an icon for horror in the annals of crime?

There are different reasons for the impact that Jack the Ripper had on the world at that time. It was primarily in England, of course, but in 1888, England was the leading power in the world. It was the height of the reign of Victoria and so, what happened in England, affected the entire world. Also, the onslaught of these terrible murders came during a time when London was in turmoil over the social structure within the environs. Newspapers were blossoming and events were chronicled in detail like never before. The masses had access to what was going on in their city, in their nation, and the world. There was another aspect to the press that helped to propel Jack the Ripper to such heights, as newspapers realized sensationalism would sell papers. And when it came to the Ripper, many of the papers succumbed to sales over social responsibility and they fed the frenzy of the murderous fiend from Whitechapel.

Jack the Ripper. His legacy lives and continues to grow. It will continue to do so until his identity is revealed and perhaps an understanding of why he committed the crimes. How likely is this revelation? Who knows? For now, only Jack knows, and he's been pretty successful at keeping secrets.

London – A City Divided

An important step in discussing the Ripper murders is understanding the environment in which they occurred. Although the murders are usually associated with the area known as Whitechapel, the victims were in other areas too, but they were all contained in the cesspool known as the East End.

London is a massive community. In the southwest region you have the areas known as Kensington and Chelsea, and proceeding in a northeasterly direction from there, you come across Buckingham Palace and Picadilly Circus. Due north is Soho and further up is the once literary arena of Bloomsbury. Continuing east, Charing Cross Road will lead you towards Trafalger Square, and south of that will be Westminster Abbey.

The City of London, which is over a square mile, is a separate legal entity than the environs known as "London". It lies in the eastern portion of the London megalopolis and is famed for its financial areas and for being the original settlement built by the Celts and conquered by the Romans. To the east of the city lies what is known as the East End of London. The Tower of London is the southernmost part of the City.

Extending north from the London Tower is the region known as the East End. It begins at Shoreditch to the north and Spitalfields to the south with Whitechapel southeastern from there. Heading further southeast would take you to the London Docks. Bethnal Green, the once renowned area is northeast of Whitechapel.

It is Whitechapel that the murders are associated with, although the victims were also found murdered in the City of London proper and the district of Spitalfields.

The East End. over-crowded, unsanitary, crime-ridden, and destitute was a haven for prostitutes, home for foreigners who had little chance to find employment, and entrenched in a poverty level that most modern people would be incapable of understanding.

At the time there was an incredible division among the West End and the East. The West was the respectable area and they felt the East held only vagrants, criminals, and foreigners. It was feared for the horrible living conditions that the residents endured, shunned for the immorality which infested the narrow streets, and despised for the level of depravity. Jack the Ripper had validated the fears of the West End, for only in such an area could a monster like that be created. After all, as a London Times editorial pointed out, the crimes committed were inconsistent with the normal English nature.

Crime in the East End was not unusual, even murder was commonplace. The conditions were so bad in the East End that normal social concerns were seldom addressed. Morality had little room for the starving masses. Living conditions were beyond the

scope of atrocious and the poor who could hold down a job were paid such poor wages that their plight was little better than the street dwellers. Although the housing was unbelievably crowded and shabby,

the rents were proportionally high because the landlords knew they could get it. When the provisions of the 1875 Artisans and Labourers Dwelling Act were enacted, many buildings were demolished as being unsanitary. This led to a housing shortage and for landlords that had tenements scheduled for demolition, there was little incentive to provide any kind of upkeep.

Life was certainly miserable in the East End. There was no illusion or hope for most of the people there with the possible exception of finding a steady job. But even that would bring in only a subsistent level, yet that would be a substantial improvement for the dwellers of Whitechapel and the nearby areas. The Church supplied an occasional meal for some and also served as boarding houses, but even those were crowded.

Here writer Blanchard Jerrold describes a charity house:

"They pass in one by one: the father with his foot sore boy-the mother with her whimpering babe in her arms, that are so lean they must hurt the flesh of the little imp. The superintendent... distributes the regulation lump of bread to the guests, and they pass on, by way of the bath-rigorously enforced for obvious reasons-to the dormitories set out like barracks, and warmed with a stove. Young and old are here-houseless, and with babes to carry forth tomorrow into the east wind and the sleet. The story is told by the coughs that crackle like a distant running fire of musketry-all over the establishment. No wonder that many of them dread the bath upon their feeble, feverish limbs: and with chests torn to rags as many of them must be."

To give an idea of the conditions in the East End, here are some startling statistics from the Rev. W.N. Davies, rector of Spitalfields, as well as information pulled from the London Country Council—in 1886.

In one alley, there were 10 houses which contained 51 rooms, nearly all 8 feet by 9 feet. These 51 rooms held 254 people. In another court, there were 6 houses and 22 rooms and 84 people. One house with 8 rooms housed 45 people.

That's an average of over 22 people per house with nearly FIVE people per (8 x 9) room.

In London at that time, there were 1.8 million people at the poverty line or below. Another million lived with one week's wage between them and pauperism.

Of the population living in the East End, 21% of them relied on the Church parishes for food and shelter.

Average life expectancy in the East End was less than 30 years.

For children, 55% of them would die before the age of five.

Jerrold tells of his first journey into Whitechapel as he accompanied Gustave Doré on a tour of the city. Their book, showcasing the wide contrasts existing in London at the time, was released as *London: A Pilgrimage.*

"We plunged into a maze of courts and narrow streets of low houses-nearly all the doors of which are open, showing kitchen fires blazing far in the interior...black pools of water under our feet...we threaded an extraordinary tangle of dark alleys where two men could just walk abreast, under the flickering lamps jutting from the ebony walls to mark the corners.

We advanced into a low, long dark room parted into boxes in which are packed the most rascally company any great city could show...it is charged with the unmistakable, overpowering damp and moldy odor, that is in every thieves' kitchen, in every common lodging house, every ragged hotel. In one box, an old man is dying of asthma, in another two fine baby boys are interlaced, sleeping till their mother brings home some supper from the hard streets."

The social consciousness regarding the East End was not completely from foreign sources such as Jerrold and Jack London. Many of the West End citizens realized the sad situation and offered their charity. But it was not enough.

Jack London, the famed American author is best remembered for his Tales of the North (Call of the Wild, White Fang), but London was an outspoken critic of the working conditions that most laborers had to face. He traveled to London and assumed the identity of a pauper and lived among the poor in the

Jack London, the American author noted more for his tales of the South Sea and Alaskan wilderness, was an avid socialist. He even ran for mayor of Oakland, California as a Socialist candidate. Two of his acclaimed works dealt with the elements of social injustice and inequality. *The Iron Heel* was a fictional story but his *The People of the Abyss* dealt with his undercover work in the East End of London. Here he narrates some of what he saw:

Jack London

On food offered workers at Whitechapel infirmary.

"...Heaped high on a huge platter in an indescribable mess—pieces of bread, chunks of grease and fat pork, the burnt skin from the outside of roasted joints, bones, in short, all the leavings from the fingers and mouths of the sick ones suffering from all manners of disease. Into this mess, the men plunged their hands, digging, pawing, turning over, examining, rejecting and scrambling for. It wasn't pretty. Pigs couldn't have done worse. But the poor devils were hungry, and they ate ravenously of the swill, and when they could eat no more, they bundled what was left into their handkerchiefs and thrust it inside their shirts."

London's first excursion into the East End.

"We went up the narrow graveled walk. On the benches on either side was arrayed a mass of miserable and distorted humanity...it was a welter of rags and filth, of all manner of loathsome skin diseases, open sores, bruises, grossness, indecency, leering monstrosities, and bestial faces. Here were a dozen women, ranging in age from 20 to 70. Next a babe, possibly of nine months, lying asleep, flat on the hard bench with neither pillow nor covering nor with any one looking after it. Next, half a dozen men, sleeping bolt upright or leaning against one another in their sleep."

As London was walking with two laborers down the streets of the East End.

"From the slimy sidewalk, they were picking up bits of orange peel, apple skin, and grape stems, and they were eating them. The pips of green gage plums they cracked between their teeth for the kernels inside. They picked up stray crumbs of bread the size of peas, apple cores so black and dirty one would not take them to be apple cores, and these things these two men took into their mouths, and chewed them and swallowed them; ...in the heart of the greatest, wealthiest, and most powerful empire the world has ever seen."

East End. He took lodging where he could, ate what they ate, and frequented the same parish charity houses and pubs as any native East Ender would do. It was a noble experiment but London had to quit sooner than he planned. The conditions were too rough for him, an experienced sailor who also lived in the wilderness of Alaska. He readily admitted defeat, but he did make numerous observations about the plight of the working poor in the East End. Here is a paraphrase from Jack London describing a family's housing.

"Here the family arises in the morning, dresses, and makes its toilet- father, mother, sons, and daughters. In the same room, shoulder to shoulder, the wife and mother cooks the breakfast. And in the same room, heavy and sickening with the exhalations of their packed bodies throughout out the night, that breakfast is eaten. The father goes to work...the mother remains with her crawling, toddling youngsters...

Here, in the evening...as many as possible pile into the one bed (if bed they have) and the surplus turns in on the floor. And this is the round of their existence, month after month, year after year, for they never get a vacation save when they are evicted.

When a child dies, and some are always bound to die since 55% of the East End children die before they are 5 years old, the body is laid out in the same room. And if they are very poor, it is kept for some time until they can bury it. During the day, it lied on the bed, during the night, when the living take the bed, the dead occupies the table, from which, in the morning, when the dead is put back into the bed, the living eat their breakfast."

The East End of London was in shambles from all fronts. It was considered a total loss in terms of morality, spirituality, economic considerations, and dropped below what many would consider even humane. It was a bomb waiting to explode as a couple of demonstrations earlier had set the stage for. It needed a trigger to bring everything to the forefront, to bring an awareness to the common laborer in the West End that his fellow workers were faced with degradable situations...it needed a catalyst to propel a joint effort of the press, the people, and the government to tackle the problem in a cohesive

Gustave Doré

manner. That trigger arrived in 1888 and he was called Jack the Ripper.

Today, as back then, there was a great deal of disagreement among the investigators on who would or should not be considered as victims of Jack the Ripper. The five victims commonly cited are those who have been labeled as such from sources in the 1930's through the 1970's. However, new documents discovered and analysis of the criminal methods have disrupted the general consensus. As mentioned previously, there were two victims that are sometimes associated with the Ripper in Emma Smith and Martha Tabram. Elizabeth Stride has come under scrutiny to determine if she was actually a victim of Jack or not. After the death of Mary Kelly, two other murders occurred in the East End, specifically Whitechapel. It occurred on July 17, 1889 and the victim was Alice McKenzie. Her throat had been cut and it appeared that there was some attempt at stomach mutilation but it wasn't as extensive as the previous murders. Two of the doctors examining McKenzie disagreed on whether she should be considered a victim of the Ripper.

Another victim was Frances Cole and the body was found two months later. Actually, all that was found was the trunk of a woman. Because of quite a bit of missing evidence, it would be hard to include this as one of the Ripper's victims but it is often associated with it.

If the bodies of McKenzie and Cole are discounted, then Kelly was the last victim and the Ripper, therefore, was never heard from again. As big of a mystery of why a person would commit such heinous crimes, is who the murderer was. Again, as with so many areas regarding Jack the Ripper, there is little consensus on who it might have been.

THE NEMESIS OF NEGLECT

"THERE FLOATS A PHANTOM ON THE SLUM'S FOUL AIR,
  SHAPING, TO EYES WHICH HAVE THE GIFT OF SEEING,
INTO THE SPECTRE OF THAT LOATHLY LAIR.
    FACE IT — FOR VAIN IS FLEEING!
RED-HANDED, RUTHLESS, FURTIVE, UNERECT,
'TIS MURDEROUS CRIME - THE NEMESIS OF NEGLECT!"

It has been generally agreed by most experts that the number of victims that can be attributed to Jack the Ripper is five. Of those, Elizabeth Stride, the first of the "double murders" has recently been under scrutiny to determine if she was actually a victim of the Ripper. There are 10-13 other victims that are alleged to have been murdered or attacked by the Ripper. Of these, some range from credible consideration while others are outright dismissed by many of the experts. They are listed here purely for reference. This overview will deal with the five victims traditionally associated with Jack the Ripper. The cause of confusion regarding the number of victims is to be expected. Since Jack the Ripper was obviously never caught (that we know of), there is no way of determining who actually fell under his knife. Another problem is that Jack seemed to be delving deeper into his mutilations as he went on, so some possible earlier victims may have been the work of this madman before he stepped up his frenzy.

The only common link between the victims is that they were all prostitutes. Some made their living in this manner while others resorted to selling sexual favors when they couldn't find any other source of income. It is believed that all were drunk at the time of the murders which wouldn't have been unusual for any of them.

The five victims in chronological order are (all occurred in 1888):

Mary Ann (Polly) Nichols	*August 31*
Annie Chapman	*September 8*
Elizabeth Stride	*September 30*
Catharine Eddowes	*September 30*
Mary Kelly	*November 9*

It is now believed that all of the victims were murdered as they faced their killer. After a great deal of debate, the popular theory now is that Jack had the women lift their skirts to allow the sexual act and he took this opportunity to put his hands around their throats and strangle them. This is in contrast to the long thought theory that Jack attacked from behind. It is then assumed he cut the victims throats after they were on the ground and it would, of course, lessen the splattering of blood. Many experts believe that Jack the Ripper had to have some kind of anatomical knowledge and the use of a knife, but not necessarily a great deal, therefore eliminating some consensus that he had to be a doctor.

No signs of intercourse was detected in any of the victims.

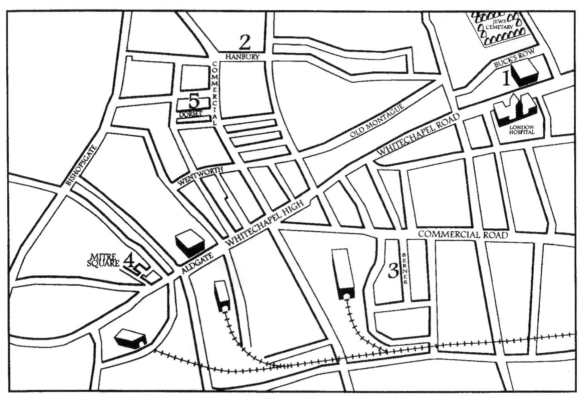

OVERVIEW OF THE RIPPER'S TERRITORY

AUGUST 31, 1888. A BODY WAS FOUND BY *GEORGE CROSS*, A MARKET PORTER, AS HE WENT TO WORK ON THAT FRIDAY MORNING AT 4:00 A.M.

CROSS ENLISTED THE AID OF ANOTHER MAN TO HELP THE WOMAN ON THE GROUND TO HER FEET. IT WAS NOT UNCOMMON TO FIND PROSTITUTES PASSED OUT IN THE STREETS IN *WHITECHAPEL*..

BUT THE *COLDNESS* OF THE BODY DROVE THE MEN IN SEARCH OF THE POLICE INSTEAD. THEY WEREN'T *SURE* AT THIS POINT, BUT THEY FELT THE WOMAN WAS DEAD. IN THE DARKNESS, THEY COULD NOT SEE THE LARGE POOL OF *BLOOD* THAT SURROUNDED HER BODY WHICH WOULD HAVE LEFT THEM NO DOUBT.

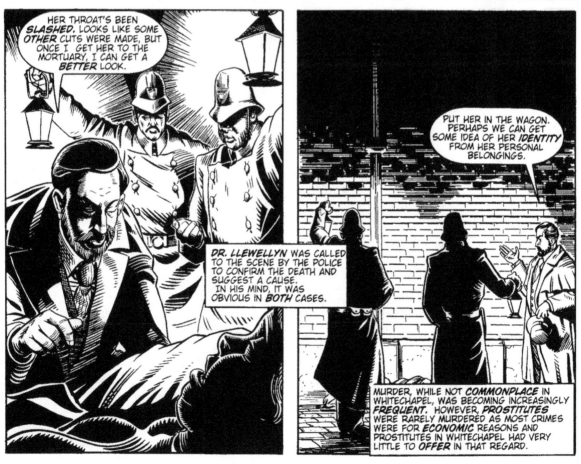

HER THROAT'S BEEN *SLASHED*. LOOKS LIKE SOME *OTHER* CUTS WERE MADE, BUT ONCE I GET HER TO THE MORTUARY, I CAN GET A *BETTER* LOOK.

PUT HER IN THE WAGON. PERHAPS WE CAN GET SOME IDEA OF HER *IDENTITY* FROM HER PERSONAL BELONGINGS.

DR. LLEWELLYN WAS CALLED TO THE SCENE BY THE POLICE TO CONFIRM THE DEATH AND SUGGEST A CAUSE. IN HIS MIND, IT WAS OBVIOUS IN *BOTH* CASES.

MURDER, WHILE NOT *COMMONPLACE* IN WHITECHAPEL, WAS BECOMING INCREASINGLY *FREQUENT*. HOWEVER, *PROSTITUTES* WERE RARELY MURDERED AS MOST CRIMES WERE FOR *ECONOMIC* REASONS AND PROSTITUTES IN WHITECHAPEL HAD VERY LITTLE TO *OFFER* IN THAT REGARD.

HER THROAT HAS BEEN CUT ALMOST FROM *EAR TO EAR*. THE CUT WAS *DEEP*, IT SEVERED HER WINDPIPE AND CUT INTO THE *SPINAL CORD*.

THE MAJOR ARTERIES WERE CUT AS WELL.

THERE DOESN'T SEEM TO BE A LOT OF BLOOD... NOT IF THE ARTERIES WERE CUT.

SHE COULD HAVE BEEN MURDERED *ELSEWHERE* AND *MOVED* HERE.

LLEWELLYN FIRST SURMISED THAT THE BODY MIGHT HAVE BEEN *MOVED* BECAUSE THERE WAS NOT ENOUGH BLOOD AROUND THE BODY TO INDICATE *ARTERIAL* BLEEDING.

BUT WHEN THE BODY WAS *PICKED UP*, THEY DISCOVERED THAT THE *CLOTHES* HAD SOAKED UP MOST OF THE BLOOD.... AN *INCREDIBLE* AMOUNT OF BLOOD.

MY GOD! SHE'S BEEN *GUTTED!*

THE VICTIM HAD BEEN ALMOST *DISEMBOWELED*. THE MAJOR GASHES IN THE STOMACH HAD DIRECTED THE BLOOD *THERE* INSTEAD OF THE NECK WOUNDS.

WHICH ALSO INDICATED THAT THE SLASHES IN THE ABDOMEN WERE DONE *PRIOR* TO THE NECK AND WERE LIKELY THE CAUSE OF DEATH.

THE POLICE QUICKLY WASHED AWAY THE BLOOD BEFORE THE MORNING SUN WOULD REVEAL THE HORRIFIC SCENE.

AND THE EVIDENCE OF THE *FIRST* VICTIM OF WHAT WAS TO BECOME THE RIPPER MURDERS...

...WAS WASHED AWAY. BUT, ALTHOUGH THE *BLOOD* WAS GONE, THE *LEGACY* HAD BEGUN.

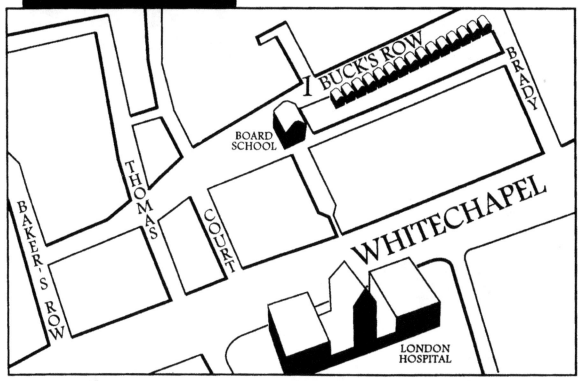

BUCK'S ROW · AUGUST 31, 1888

The woman found at Buck's Row was known as Polly Nichols, although her real name was Mary Ann Walker Nichols. Her father was a locksmith and Polly married when she was 18. However, after five children, she and her husband, William Nichols, divorced. Polly's children stayed with their father and her own father while she worked a variety of jobs and lived with different men. Always attempting to better herself, Polly struggled to maintain a consistent job whether it was as a servant or in the workhouses, but alcohol was her continual downfall.

When her body was discovered, it was the third murder in the area known as Whitechapel. Although the first two victims are not commonly associated with Jack the Ripper, at the time of Polly's death, the fervor over another victim was quite loud. With the death of Polly Nichols, the concern was now over the death of three women and there was no separation of the prior two victims and Nichols, who would eventually be listed as the first of the Ripper victims.

In April, Emma Smith had been attacked. She claimed it was by four men but could not describe them. However, four hours prior, she was seen talking to just one man. She had her ear cut but the major injury to her was internal from an object being forced into her. She died of peritonitis. Because of the claim of the four men, most experts dismiss her as a victim of the Ripper. However, the next prostitute

to die in Whitechapel would fit, according to some Ripperologists, in the pattern of Jack the Ripper.

Martha Tabram's body was found on August 7, in the George Yard. This area would be in approximately the center of the five "official" Ripper victims. She had been stabbed 39 times and her clothes were pulled up as if to engage in intercourse, but there is no proof that she did. Tabram was a prostitute and there were many similarities to the upcoming crimes that have led many experts to seriously consider her as a Ripper victim. Although her body didn't suffer the mutilation as the others, some surmise that the Ripper showed an increased tendency with each murder and therefore Tabram's body could fit in.

From Scotland Yard, Detective-Inspector Frederick Abberline, was called into the investigation of Polly Nichols. It is important to remember that for the residents of the East End, this was the third murder and naturally, they were apprehensive about a murdering spree being initiated. There were little clues to suggest who the murderer was and there were no witnesses. The killer obviously must have had blood on his hands and possibly his clothes, but because there were so many slaughterhouses in the East End, a man walking with blood on him was not abnormally suspicious. In addition to not having a suspect, Abberline and the police also had to deal with no apparent motive for the crime. Without an

A sketch of the body of Martha Tabram from the Illustrated Police News. She was often called "Turner" as she was living with a man named Turner.

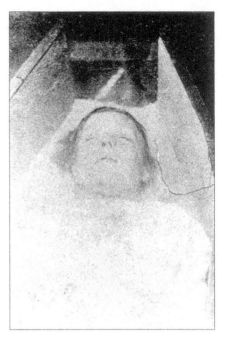

(above) The mortuary photograph of Polly Nichols.

(above) The mortuary photograph of Martha Tabrum.

(right) The discovery of the body of Mary Ann (Polly) Nichols by PC John Neil. Nichols is generally considered by most to be the first "Ripper" victim.

Insector Frederick Abberline

Abberline is often considered the primary investigator of the Ripper murders. He came on the scene after the death of Polly Nichols, however, at that time, Nichols was considered the third victim. Abberline felt that Tabrum as a Ripper victim had merit.

Abberline was known for his vast knowledge of Whitechapel and the criminal element there but he was never able to provide an answer to who was Jack the Ripper.

POLLY NICHOLS

apparent motive or witnesses, the police had little to go on. The scientific methods that we take for granted now did not exist then. It would be nearly two decades before fingerprinting began to be used. And, most importantly, murders of this type were highly unusual. In previous serial type killings, there was an apparent motive in robbing the victims, but that did not apply here. The police were immersed in an unusual and unfamiliar territory.

As the police canvassed the area, they did come with a lead... a man named Jack Pizer. Pizer was nicknamed Leather Apron because he always wore one. Many of the prostitutes were in fear of Pizer because he would beat them if they didn't concede with his demands. As the police looked for Pizer (who was hiding with relatives once notified of the police's interest), the press followed the same lead. The newspapers, anxious for any kind of information regarding these murders, quickly jumped on the possibility that the killer was Leather Apron. Soon, the papers' headlines screamed of the mysterious leather apron who prowled Whitechapel at night with his long knife. Rumors abounded about his forays into the foggy night searching for his next victim. Pizer undoubtedly was more worried about the mobs attacking him than the police capturing him and he remained hidden. Leather Apron grew in stature as the killer, especially when just over a week later, another victim had been found.

From THE LONDON TIMES,
  September 3, 1888
Inquest regarding Mary Ann Nichols
Subject- Dr. Henry Llewellyn at his arrival in Buck's Row.

On reaching Buck's-row he found deceased lying flat on her back on the pathway, her legs being extended. Deceased was quite dead, and she had severe injuries to her throat. Her hands and wrists were cold, but the lower extremities were quite warm. Witness examined her chest and felt the heart. It was dark at the time. He should say the deceased had not been dead more than half an hour. He was certain that the injuries to the neck were not self-inflicted. There was very little blood round the neck, and there were no marks of any struggle, or of blood as though the body had been dragged. Witness gave the police directions to take the body to the mortuary, where he would make another examination. About an hour afterwards he was sent for by the inspector to see the other injuries he had discovered on the body. Witness went, and saw that the abdomen was cut very extensively. That morning he made a post mortem examination of the body. It was that of a female of about 40 or 45 years. Five of the teeth were missing, and there was a slight laceration of the tongue. There was a bruise running along the lower part of the jaw on the right side of the face. That might have been caused by a blow from a fist or pressure from a thumb. There was a circular bruise on the left side of the face, which also might have been inflicted by the pressure of the fingers. On the left side of the neck, about 1in. below the jaw, there was an incision about 4 in. in length, and ran from a point immediately below the ear. On the same side, but an inch below, and commencing about 1 in. in front of it, was a circular incision, which terminated in a point about 3 in. below the right jaw. That incision completely severed all the tissues down to the vertebrae. The large vessels of the neck on both sides were severed. The incision was about 8in. in length. The cuts must have been caused by a long-bladed knife, moderately sharp, and used with great violence. No blood was found on the breast, either of the body or clothes. There were no injuries about the body until just below the lower part of the abdomen. Two or three inches from the left side was a wound running in a jagged manner. The wound was a very deep one, and the tissues were cut through. There were several incisions running across the abdomen. There were also three or four similar cuts, running downwards, on the right side, all of which had been caused by a knife which had been used violently and downwards. The injuries were from left to right, and might have been done by a left-handed person. All the injuries had been caused by the same instrument.

No. 1423.—Vol. 55.   SEPTEMBER 8, 1888

THE ·PENNY·
ILLUSTRATED · PAPER
AND ·ILLUSTRATED TIMES

REGISTERED AT THE GENERAL POST-OFFICE AS A NEWSPAPER.

London: Printed and Published at the Office, 13, Milford-lane, Strand, in the Parish of St. Clement Danes, in the County of Middlesex, by Thomas Fox, 10, Milford-lane, Strand, aforesaid

SKETCHES AT THE INQUEST

P.C. NIEL J. 97.   Dr. LLEWELLYN   INSPR. HELSON   THE CORONER

East London has a terror that must be stamped out. We illustrate on this page, and describe in another, Police-Constable Niel's discovery of murdered Mary Ann Nicholls in Buck's-row, Whitechapel, on the early morning of August the Thirty-first. The crime has so many points of similarity with the murders of the two other women in the same neighbourhood—one, Martha Turner, as recently as Aug. 7, and the other less than twelve months previously—that the police admit their belief that the three crimes are the work of one individual. All three women were of the same class, and each of them was so poor that robbery could have formed no motive for the crime. The three murders were committed within a distance of 200 yards of each other

THE WHITECHAPEL MYSTERY.

P.C. NEIL FINDING THE BODY OF POLLY NICHOLS IN BUCK'S ROW

ANNIE CHAPMAN WAS ONCE A BEAUTIFUL YOUNG GIRL. HER FUTURE HUSBAND, FRED CHAPMAN, CALLED HER HIS "DARK ANGEL".

BUT TO LOOK AT HER NOW, IT WOULD BE HARD TO IMAGINE ANY ANALOGY OF ANGEL BEING APPLIED TO HER.

SHE WAS HEADED FOR A GOOD LIFE. WIFE OF A SOLDIER WHO WOULD COLLECT A STEADY PENSION, THEY LIVED IN THE BUSTLING BOROUGH OF WINDSOR.

BUT AFTER THE BIRTH OF THEIR FIRST CHILD, A DEFORMED BOY AND THEN THEIR SECOND, A GIRL WHO WOULD EVENTUALLY BE CONFINED TO AN INSTITUTION, THE MARRIAGE FELL APART.

IT'S LATE, ANNIE. AREN'T YOU GOING TO BED?

I DON'T HAVE THE MONEY.

FRED AND ANNIE SEPARATED. AND ANNIE, FINDING HER SOLACE IN GIN, COULD NOT HOLD DOWN A STEADY JOB.

YOU KNOW THE RULES. NO MONEY, NO BED.

BUT I'M GOOD FOR IT, YOU KNOW THAT.

AND WHEN SHE COULD NOT FIND AN INCOME FROM HONEST WORK, SHE GAVE HERSELF AS DID SO MANY OTHER WOMEN OF THE TIMES.

I'LL BE BACK WITH THE MONEY.

I'LL GET IT SOMEHOW.

AND THAT WAS THE LAST TIME THAT ANNIE CHAPMAN WOULD VENTURE INTO THE NIGHT TO GIVE MOMENTARY PLEASURE TO A PAYING CUSTOMER.

THAT MORNING, AROUND 5:00 ON SEPTEMBER 8, ANNIE FINALLY *SUCCEEDED* IN FINDING A POTENTIAL CUSTOMER.

A WITNESS WHO WALKED BY HEARD ANNIE HAGGLING WITH THE MAN WHO HE DID NOT PAY MUCH ATTENTION TO. IT WAS ALWAYS BETTER TO MIND ONE'S OWN BUSINESS IN THE EAST END.

ANNIE WAS IN ONE OF HER FAVORITE SPOTS, THE YARD BEHIND *29 HANBURY STREET*. EVEN THOUGH IT WAS OUTSIDE, FEW PEOPLE PAID ATTENTION TO WHAT WENT ON IN THE EARLY MORNING HOURS.

SHE WAS FOUND ONLY 30 MINUTES LATER. HER HANDKER-CHIEF WAS TIGHTLY *KNOTTED* AROUND HER THROAT...

...THIS BEING THE *ONLY* THING THAT KEPT HER HEAD ATTACHED. THE FRONTAL INCISION HAD TRACKED FROM ONE EAR TO THE NECK, SLICING THROUGH THE VETERBRAE.

TO THOSE FIRST ON THE SCENE, IT SEEMED UNREAL. WHAT WAS *FIRST* THOUGHT TO BE RIPPED CLOTHING LAYING ON HER SHOULDER...

...WAS LATER TO BE SHOWN TO BE HER *INTESTINES* THAT WERE PULLED OUT AND GENTLY LAID NEXT TO HER HEAD.

LAID CAREFULLY AT HER FEET WERE THE WEDDING BANDS WHICH SHE WORE IN HONOR OF HER HUSBAND WHO HAD DIED SOME MONTHS AGO...

...AND SOME NEWLY MINTED FARTHINGS. IN HER PROFESSION, SHE HAD SOLD HER BODY... AND THIS WOULD BE HER *LAST* PAYMENT.

GHASTLY MURDER

IN THE EAST-END.

DREADFUL MUTILATION OF A WOMAN.

Capture : Leather Apron

Another murder of a character even more diabolical than that perpetrated in Buck's Row, on Friday week, was discovered in the same neighbourhood, on Saturday morning. At about six o'clock a woman was found lying in a back yard at the foot of a passage leading to a lodging-house in a Old Brown's Lane, Spitalfields. The house is occupied by a Mrs. Richardson, who lets it out to lodgers, and the door which admits to this passage, at the foot of which lies the yard where the body was found, is always open for the convenience of lodgers. A lodger named Davis was going down to work at the time mentioned and found the woman lying on her back close to the flight of steps leading into the yard. Her throat was cut in a fearful manner. The woman's body had been completely ripped open, and the heart and other organs laying about the place, and portions of the entrails round the victim's neck. An excited crowd gathered in front of Mrs. Richardson's house and also round the mortuary in old Montague Street, whither the body was quickly conveyed. As the body lies in the rough coffin in which it has been placed in the mortuary —the same coffin in which the unfortunate Mrs. Nicholls was first placed—it presents a tearful sight. The body is that of a woman about 45 years of age. The height is exactly five feet. The complexion is fair, with wavy dark brown hair; the eyes are blue, and two lower teeth have been knocked out. The nose is rather large and prominent.

HANBURY STREET · SEPTEMBER 8, 1888

Less than half a mile from Buck's Row, another body was found...that of Annie Chapman, sometimes referred to as Dark Annie. Found by a lodger, John Davis, who went into the street to get help. The police report was succinct regarding the atrocity: "Lying on her back, dead, left arm resting on left breast, legs drawn up, abducted, small intestines and flap of the abdomen lying on right side above right shoulder attached by a cord with the rest of the intestines inside the body; two flaps of skin from the lower part of the abdomen lying in a large quantity of blood above the left shoulder; throat cut deeply from left and back in jagged manner right around the throat."

There was a scarf around Annie's neck and at first it was presumed that the killer had wrapped it around in order to keep the head attached. Later reports however, indicated that Annie was wearing the scarf previous to her murder. As the police looked around the ground, they had to contend with the large number of "sight see-ers" who were milling around before a large enough force could successfully clear them out. One of the startling discoveries was that of a leather apron lying near the water tap. A description of a suspicious man was given also. It matched fairly close to that of Jack Pizer.

Pizer was apprehended two days later. A

madness swept the East End as it was assumed the ghastly murderer had been caught. However, Pizer was soon let go because he had witnesses to confirm his whereabouts when the murders were committed. Another suspect was picked up, William Piggott, who resembled the description of Pizer. He had been spotted in a pub with bloodstained clothing. The police had their doubts about Piggott but decided to keep him in custody. Within hours of being locked up, however, Piggott exhibited some strange behavior and was sent to an insane asylum at Bow. He was not Jack the Ripper.

Annie Chapman, also known as Annie Siffey, seemed to headed to a life of contentment. Married in her early 20's to a coachman named John Chapman and settled down in Berkeley Square. They had three children before they moved to Windsor in 1881 where Chapman assumed a position as Head Coachman. But it was then that Annie's life began a downward spiral.

The oldest daughter died in 1882 of meningitis. With the troubles the couple faced with their children (their only son being a cripple), the marriage of John and Annie Chapman fell apart. John was a heavy drinker but still managed to send support money to Annie after they split. But in 1886, John died from complications of his alcoholism. One of Annie's closest friends, Amelia Palmer, said that the

ANNIE CHAPMAN

death of John hit Annie hard and that Annie "she has seemed to give way altogether."

The case of Annie Chapman is one that has been hotly contested by many of the Ripper experts. The common fable of her rings and the coins being placed at her feet is under dispute and police reports indicate no such actions. In fact, the missing rings were a reason for the police to check out the local pawn shops in case they were sold. However, the rings were valueless and perhaps the murdered realized that later. It seems that the story of the rings being placed at Chapman's feet was initiated by the press who often embellished the story for their own gain...mainly that of sensationalism to sell papers.

Chapman was the first of the victims to have any of her organs removed and the manner in which they were cut out led authorities to believe that the work was of a skillful surgeon or at least someone with advanced medical knowledge. This is a proposition that gained quite a bit of attention in the lore of the Ripper specialists and opened up a wide spectrum of speculation that the Ripper had to be a doctor or the like. Most of the Ripperologists claim that the level of skill exhibited by Jack does not necessitate a great deal of medical knowledge, certainly not at the level of surgical precision.

A news report from **THE MANCHESTER GUARDIAN**
A typical story regarding the suspect known as Leather Apron.
(Note: this is a condensed version)

...to a mysterious being bearing the name of "Leather Apron," concerning whom a number of stories have for a week or more been current in Whitechapel. Of this individual the following description is given:

The distinguishing feature of his costume is a leather apron, which he always wears, and from which he gets his nickname. His expression is sinister, and seems to be full of terror for the women who describe it. His eyes are small and glittering. His lips are usually parted in a grin, which is not only not reassuring, but excessively repellent. He is a slippermaker by trade, but does not work. His business is blackmailing women late at night. A number of men in Whitechapel follow this interesting profession. His name nobody knows, but all are united in the belief that he is a Jew or of Jewish parentage, his face being of a marked Hebrew type. But the most singular characteristic of the man is the universal statement that in moving about he never makes any noise. What he wears on his feet the women do not know, but all agree that he moves noiselessly. His uncanny peculiarity to them is that they never see him or know of his presence until he is close by them. "Leather Apron" never by any chance attacks a man. He runs away on the slightest appearance of rescue. He ranges all over London, and rarely assails the same woman twice.

The whole of the East End up till a late hour on Saturday night was in a state of consternation, at the latest and what undoubtedly is the most horrible of a series of murders which have taken place within so small an area and during so short a period. All day nothing else was talked of, even by men who are hardened to seeing a great deal that is brutal. Strong, buxom, muscular women seemed to move in fear and trembling, declaring that they would not dare to venture in the streets unaccompanied by their husbands. What has added to the frantic state of the inhabitants of Whitechapel is the fact that the murder was committed in broad daylight and in a street sufficiently near to the Spitalfields Market as to be, at the time in question, a busy thoroughfare. Old residents remarked that Whitechapel and Spitalfields had never borne a particularly good name, but now it had become untenable and unsafe.

During the period of greatest excitement two men were arrested for trifling offenses this morning, and on each occasion a maddened crowd ran after the police shouting "The murderer's caught!" Another man, injured in a quarrel, and who was carried to the police station on a stretcher, received similar attention, the crowd fairly mobbing the station and refusing to disperse. Two men who were passing through Brick Lane were denounced by the crowd as the murderers and were attacked. They called upon the police for protection and were taken to Bethnal Green Station and there released. There was also a report current during the day that another woman had been murderously attacked by a man with a knife, and that the assailant was the murderer of Chapman. It, however, transpired that the man who was arrested was blind, and that in an ungovernable fit of passion he had in Spitalfields market inflicted several wounds with a knife upon a woman who led him about.

Later particulars state that a theory exists that "Leather Apron" is more or less a mythical personage, and that he is not responsible for the terrible crimes with which his name has been associated. All the same, the details of his appearance have been widely circulated with a view to his early apprehension, and all the police in the vicinity are on the look-out for him.

Newspaper Illustrations about the Ripper murders.

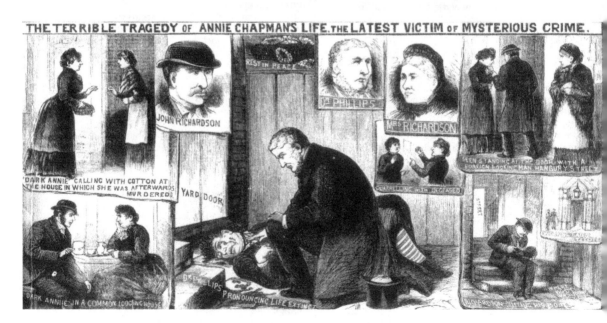

SUNDAY, SEPTEMBER 30. TO MOST OF THE EAST ENDERS, IT WAS STILL SATURDAY NIGHT EVEN THOUGH THE TIME HAD SLIPPED INTO THE NEXT DAY.

A MERCHANT, *LOUIS DIEMSCHUTZ*, SELLER OF COSTUME JEWELRY, WAS RETURNING AFTER A SUCCESSFUL DAY AT THE MARKET ON *WESTOW HILL*.

HE LONGED TO PUT HIS HORSE AND CART AWAY TO JOIN THE FESTIVITIES AT THE WORKING MAN'S CLUB. THE NOISE AND LAUGHTER FUELED HIS THIRST.

HIS HORSE SHIED AWAY AND *REFUSED* TO FINISH THE FINAL PART OF THE LONG DAY'S JOURNEY.

DIEMSCHUTZ COULD MAKE OUT A FIGURE IN THE SHADOWS. HE ASSUMED IT WAS YET ANOTHER DRUNK, AN ALL TOO COMMON SIGHT.

LEAVING HIS BUGGY, HE WENT TO WAKE THE DRUNKEN WOMAN AND SEND HER ON HER WAY.

THE *DARKNESS* AT FIRST OBSCURED HIS VISION. HE COULD SEE IT WAS DEFINITELY A WOMAN BUT SHE WASN'T STIRRING.

INSIDE THE CLUB, DIEMSCHUTZ ASKED FOR A *LAMP* SO HE COULD TRY AGAIN TO ROUSE THE DRUNKEN WOMAN. PERHAPS THE LIGHT WOULD *HELP*.

CURIOUS OF WHAT DIEMSCHUTZ WAS UP TO, SOME OF THE PEOPLE AT THE CLUB CAME OUT INTO THE FRESH AIR. MORE THAN LIKELY, THEY WERE INTERESTED IN SEEING *WHO* DRANK THEMSELVES INTO A STUPOR *THIS* TIME.

SUDDENLY, A *SCREAM* PIERCED THE NIGHT. IT WAS DIEMSCHUTZ.

THE PATRONS OF THE BAR CAME *RUNNING* OUT TO FIND WHAT HAD STARTLED DIEMSCHUTZ.

THE LIGHT OF DIEMSCHUTZ'S LAMP SHOWED THE BODY OF *ELIZABETH STRIDE*. HER THROAT HAD BEEN SLASHED-- DEEP, VIRTUALLY *SEVERING* THE HEAD.

AS THEY WATCHED THE BLOOD SEEP FROM THE BODY, UNKNOWN TO THEM, IT WAS ONLY THE *FIRST* MURDER OF THE NIGHT FOR *JACK THE RIPPER*.

THE DISCOVERY IN BERNER STREET

THE DISCOVERY IN MITRE SQUARE

**LONDON'S REIGN OF TERROR: SCENES OF
SUNDAY MORNING'S MURDERS IN THE EAST-END.**

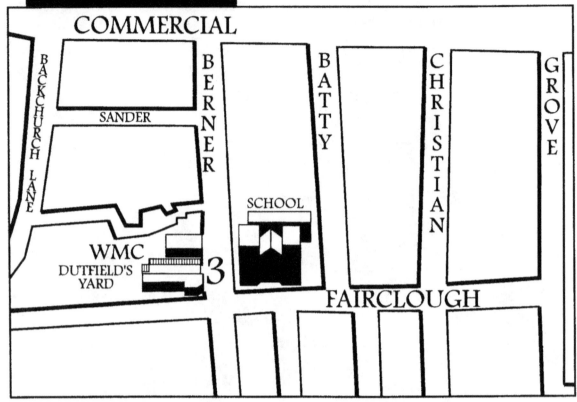

COMMERCIAL

BACKCHURCH LANE

SANDER

BERNER

BATTY

CHRISTIAN

GROVE

SCHOOL

WMC
DUTFIELD'S
YARD

3

FAIRCLOUGH

BERNER STREET · SEPTEMBER 30, 1888

The body of Elizabeth Stride was taken to St. George's Mortuary. In order to obtain a clue to her identify, Inspector Reid did an examination of the body. He guessed her age at 42 (she was actually 44), her height was 5'2, and her front teeth were missing. There were no clues revealing her name in her personal effects.

The next day, the body was identified by Mary Malcolm as that of her sister, Elizabeth Watts. But the police were suspicious of Malcolm's identification because of discrepancies and when the real Elizabeth Watts showed up, they knew they still had to identify the body. Because she was fairly well known in the area, the true identity came quickly and Long Liz, as she was often called, was properly identified.. However, Liz had been leading a life of lies and soon, all that would be revealed as well.

Born as Elisabeth Gustafsdotter in Sweden to a farming family, she moved to the city of Gothenburg when she was 17. Within the next five years, she was arrested as a prostitute and also admitted a few times to the hospital for venereal diseases. After delivering a still born child when she was 22, Elisabeth moved to London. She married a carpenter named John Stride in 1869 and was 27 at the time. According to Elisabeth, it was after the marriage that tragedy struck. Eliasbeth claimed she

had borne nine children altogether but there is no records verifying this. She said that her husband and some of her children had died in the tragedy of the Princess Alice which was a pleasure steamer that sunk in 1878. At the time, it was considered one of the most horrible disasters known even though few people have heard of it in today's world, but nearly 700 people had lost their life. In addition to losing her husband and children, it was during this tragedy that Elisabeth also lost her front teeth because of an injury suffered at the time.

The truth was revealed later. Elisabeth had never been on the Princess Alice. Her husband had died penniless in a workhouse and as for her children, there were none to be found. A post mortem inspection of her mouth showed no injury and the teeth were simply gone because of neglect and poor hygiene. Not much is recorded about her activities except that she drank quite a bit and was a frequent guest at the police station for being drunk and disorderly. However, when sober, Liz was said to be good natured and most felt she was generally a good person. It was the desire for drink that Liz would occasionally turn to prostitution and it was not her common trade.

The murder of Elizabeth Stride has been questioned by many Ripperologists as whether it

ELIZABETH STRIDE

should truly be considered one of the Ripper murders. Obviously, the major reason is that it was committed the same night as another murder, that of Catherine Eddowes, whose death fit in more with the typical murder associated with Jack the Ripper. Stride had shown no signs of strangulation which were present in the other victims. There were no mutilations on the body and the cut across Elizabeth's neck was of a different nature than the others and one of the doctors examining Elizabeth claimed that it was not a long knife, as in the other murders, but rather a short one. However, the general consensus among the experts is that Jack was interrupted in his attack on Elizabeth Stride and that's why her killing doesn't quite fit the standard profile. This also explains why a second murder was committed right afterwards.

There were quite a number of witnesses regarding Elizasbeth's final night. but they vary considerably to lend credence to any one of them being strongly considered as the Ripper. However, one account which was popularized in the newspapers of the time has continued to be identified with Jack the Ripper even today. Mrs. Fanny Mortimor identified a young man, about the age of 30, dressed in black and carrying a small black bag. Even though the man who Mortimor saw came into the police station to clear his identity the next day, the indelible image of the stalking figure in black complete with bag continues as the image of Jack the Ripper portrayed by most.

YOURS TRULY, JACK THE RIPPER

There were many letters to the police claiming to be the murderer and two of the most famous letters received by the police were signed Jack the Ripper. Even though there is considerable doubt that these letters are genuine, the name has stuck with the murderer over the last century. It is obvious that once the name was attached, other fraudulent claims would be made utilizing the same name.

The first letter was postmarked just days before the double murders. It read:

Dear Boss,
I keep on hearing the police have caught me but they won't fix me just yet. I have laughed when they look so clever and talk about being on the right track. That joke about leather Apron gave me real fits. I am down on whores and I shan't quit rippin them till I do get buckled. Grand work the last job was. I gave the ladey no time to squeal. How can they catch me now. I love my work and want to start again. You will soon hear of me with my funny little games. I saved some of the proper red stuff in a ginger beer bottle over the last job to write with but it went thick like glue and I can't use it. Red ink is fit enought I hope ha ha. The next job I do I shall clip the lady's ears off and send to the police officers just for jolly wouldn't you. Keep this letter back till I do a bit more work, then give it out straight. My knife is nice and sharp I want to get to work right away if I get a chance. Good luck.
Yours Truly,
Jack the Ripper

Don't mind me giveing the trade name.
Wasn't good enought to post this before I got all the red ink off my hands curse it.
No luck yet they say I am a doctor now ha ha.

Some credence is given to this letter because it appeared to some experts that Jack the Ripper did indeed try and cut the ears off both Stride and Eddowes.

The second letter from "Jack the Ripper" is probably the most famous as it was rumored to have been the work of whomever committed the double murders. It was actually a post card and instead of to the police, it was sent to the Central News Agency. It was posted on September 30th, the day of the double murders, which gave it quite a bit of validity as the general information regarding the murders was not yet publicly released.

I was not coddling dear old Boss when I gave you the tip. You'll hear about Saucy Jack's work tomorrow. Double event this time. Number one squealed a bit. Couldn't finish straight off. Had not time to get ears for police. Thanks for keeping last letter back till I got to work again.

Jack the Ripper

Many of the doubters as to the authenticity of these letters claim that it would have been easy for a member of the press to have received information in time to postmark the second postcard. The sensationalism over actual letters from the murder with the name of jack the 'Ripper surely would have sold a considerable amount of newspapers. So, are the letters genuine? Again, with the Ripper, there are no easy answers and the more experts you talk to, the more varying opinions you are sure to receive. Nonetheless, these letters are important and crucial in the Ripper lore.

25. Sept. 1888.

Dear Boss,

I keep on hearing the police have caught me but they wont fix me just yet. I have laughed when they look so clever and talk about being on the right track. That joke about Leather apron gave me real fits. I am down on whores and I shant quit ripping them till I do get buckled. Grand work the last job ~~was~~ I gave the lady no time to squeal. How can they catch me now. I love my work and want to start again. You will soon hear of me with my funny little games. I saved some of the proper red stuff in a ginger beer bottle over the last job to write with but it went thick like glue and I cant use it. Red ink is fit enough I hope <u>ha. ha</u>. The next job I do I shall clip the ladys ears off and send to the

THE HISTORY OF THE LAST VICTIMS OF THE MYSTERIOUS MONSTER OF THE EAST-END.

(Below) Posted notice.
(right) Mortuary photograph of Elizabeth Stride

POLICE NOTICE.

TO THE OCCUPIER.

On the mornings of Friday, 31st August, Saturday 8th, and Sunday, 30th September, 1888, Women were murdered in or near Whitechapel, supposed by some one residing in the immediate neighbourhood. Should you know of any person to whom suspicion is attached, you are earnestly requested to communicate at once with the nearest Police Station.

Metropolitan Police Office,
30th September, 1888.

Printed by M'Corquodale & Co. Limited, "The Armoury," Southwark.

POLICE *THE ILLUSTRATED* NEWS

LAW COURTS AND WEEKLY RECORD

THE BERNER ST VICTIM.

INQUEST ON FIFTH VICTIM AT ST GEORGES IN THE EAST

INSPECTOR REID

TWO MORE WHITECHAPEL HORRORS. WHEN WILL THE MURDERER BE CAPTURED?

BACK OF BERNER STREET

POLICE CONSTABLE WATKINS SIGNALLING FOR ASSISTANCE

MITRE SQUARE ALDGATE

THE SCENE ON SUNDAY IN BERNER STREET

FINDING THE BODY IN MITRE SQUARE.

THE FIFTH VICTIM OF THE WHITECHAPEL FIEND.

FINDING THE MUTILATED BODY MITRE SQARE.

HER NAME WAS *KATHERINE EDDOWES* BUT SHE HAD GIVEN HER NAME AS *MARY ANN KELLY.*

THE POLICE, AS CUSTOMARY, RELEASED THE DRUNKEN PROSTITUTES AFTER THEY SOBERED UP.

PC *GEORGE HALL* REMEMBERED THE WOMAN AS WELL AS THE *LAST* WORDS THAT SHE SPOKE...

GOOD *NIGHT,* OLD COCK.

IN LESS THAN AN *HOUR,* HER MUTILATED BODY WOULD BE DISCOVERED AND SHE WOULD FOREVER BE CONNECTED WITH ANOTHER VICTIM, *ELIZABETH STRIDE,* IN WHAT RIPPEROLOGISTS CALL THE *DOUBLE EVENT.*

THE BODY OF CATHERINE EDDOWES FOUND IN MITRE SQUARE WAS THE ONLY VICTIM IN THE CITY OF LONDON. IT WAS THEREFORE, UNDER A *DIFFERENT* JURISDICTION THAN THE FIRST THREE.

AND, IN A MORE *GRUESOME* DEPARTURE, EDDOWES WAS THE FIRST TO HAVE HER *FACE* MUTILATED.

THE POLICE, ALREADY PRIMED TO BE ON THE LOOKOUT FOR SUSPICIOUS CHARACTERS, SEARCHED THE AREA.

OF *ALL* THE VICTIMS, THIS WAS THE ONE THAT HAD THE BEST CHANCE TO REVEAL THE KILLER KNOWN AS *JACK THE RIPPER*.

BUT IN A TIME WITH NO RADIOS OR POLICE CARS, AND THE LACK OF AN IDENTIFIED SUSPECT, THE POLICE HAD *LITTLE* CHANCE.

A PIECE OF *APRON* WAS FOUND AND SOME CLAIMED IT MATCHED THE TEAR OF EDDOWE'S APRON. THE CLOTH WAS RUMORED TO HAVE BEEN THERE LESS THAN *FIVE MINUTES*.

BUT MORE IMPORTANTLY, WAS A *MESSAGE*. ALTHOUGH NEVER PROVED IT WAS THE WORK OF THE *RIPPER*, IT WOULD FASCINATE RIPPEROLOGISTS FOR OVER 100 YEARS.

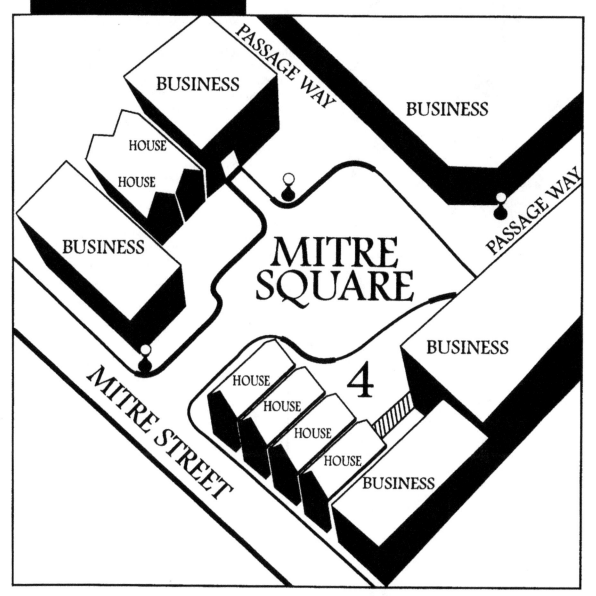

MITRE SQUARE · SEPTEMBER 30, 1888

Catherine Eddowes had lived a rough life and although she is commonly associated with being a prostitute, many of her friends insist that she never participated in selling her body. She was poor and could be sometimes considered a vagrant and even an occasional drunk, but she was not a prostitute. The truth of the matter will never be clear.

Catherine was one of 11 children and her mother died of tuberculosis when she was 13. Catherine was sent to live with her aunt as all the children were dispersed to relatives, work houses, or as domestic servants. After a few months with her aunt, Catherine went to Birmingham to live with an uncle. It was there that she met Thomas Conway when she had just turned 16. They never married but lived together for 20 years and had three children. Catherine even had Thomas' initials tattooed on her arm (T.C.) The couple moved to London and because of the bouts they had with alcohol, they separated in 1880. The following year, Catherine met John Kelly in a lodging house and they moved in together. Again, she didn't marry but she did use Kelly as her last name often and her first name was usually referred to as Kate.

John Kelly and Kate worked a variety of jobs to make ends meet. As with many of the East Enders, finding a steady job was nearly impossible. The landlord reported that their rent payments were

morning, I wandered round in the crowds that had been gathered by the talk about the two fresh murders. I stood and looked at the very spot where my poor old gal had laid with her body all cut to pieces and I never knew it.

Yesterday morning, I began to be worried a bit...I came in here (Cooney's) and asked for Kate, she had not been in. I sat down on the bench by the table and picked up a Star paper. I read down the page a bit, and my eye caught the name of Burrell. It looked familiar, but I didn't think where I had seen it until I came to the word pawnticket. Then it came over me all at once. The tin box, the two pawntickets...But could Kate have lost them? I read a little further. 'The woman had the letters T.C. in India ink, on her arm.' Man, you could have knocked me down with a feather! It was my Kate..."

Perhaps one of the most interesting aspects regarding Catherine Eddowes is the name that she gave at the police station. She said her last name was Kelly, even though she had not married John Kelly. The next victim of the Ripper would also have the name of Kelly.

regular, they seldom were out late at night, but there were a few instances where Kate was drinking too heavily, but it was nothing unusual. Kate kept in touch with her daughter, Annie, but it was usually to ask her for money. Kate's other two children did not let Kate know where they lived.

On the night of her murder, Kate and John Kelly had pawned some boots and other clothing. The pawn tickets had initially caused some confusion when her body was found because one was in the name of Burrell and the other was listed under Anne Kelly which was a name Kate sometimes used. After using the money from the pawn for food, John went to find work and Kate was scheduled to visit her daughter. The breakfast they shared was the last time John saw Kate alive.

It is known now that Kate never visited her daughter yet somehow she managed to come up with some money as she was found drunk and taken to the police station where she was incarcerated until sober. Her body would be found about an hour later. In regards to the lettering on the wall when the police were searching for clues, it was almost immediately washed away. It read something akin to "The Juwes are not The men That will be Blamed for nothing." What it actually means and how it ties into the Ripper murders will forever be a question. Some experts feel it was a significant clue whereas others claim it has no place in the study of Jack the Ripper.

Kate was identified by John Kelly and this abbreviated testimony from an interview gives a chilling recollection of his finding out about the victim being Kate.

"When she didn't come at night, I didn't worry for I thought her daughter might have asked her to stay over Sunday with her. So, on Sunday

One of the most famous letters from "Jack the Ripper" was not actually signed as being from Jack. It was addressed to George Lusk, head of the Whitechapel Vigilance Committee and was delivered with a portion of a kidney. Since Eddowes was missing one of her kidneys, the popular consensus was that it was her kidney that was delivered with the letter which is now known as being the infamous "From Hell" letter and was sent on October 16th.

From Hell

Mr. Lusk
    Sir
      I send you half the kidne I took from one woman prasarved it for you tother piece I fried and ate it was very nise I may send you the bloody knif that took it out if you only wate a whil longer
signed
        Catch me when you can Mishter Lusk

There was another letter that was signed "Jack the Ripper" and this was delivered to Dr. Openshaw, Pathological Curator of the London Hospital Museum who testified that the kidney delivered to Mr. Lusk was indeed a kidney from a female woman about the age of 45 and had been removed within the last three weeks. It also showed signs of Bright's disease, which Eddowes had also been inflicted with.

Old boss you was rite it was the left kidny i was goin to hoperate agin close to your ospitle just as i was going to dror mi nife along of er bloomin throte them cusses of coppers spolit the game but i guess i wil be on the job soon and will send you another bit of innerds

Jack the Ripper

O have you seen the devle with his mikerscope and scalpul a-lookin at a kidney with a slide cocked up.

(upper left) The infamous "From Hell" letter sent to George Lusk (pictured below) who was head of the Whitechapel Vigilance committee. This was the letter that was sent along with a human kidney.

(lower left). The follow up letter sent to Dr.. Openshaw who examined the kidney that was sent to Lusk.

There were a number of letters sent to the police and they spent a great deal of time and energy in their attempts to find if any were truly genuine. For the most part, the letters are discounted as being actually from "Jack the Ripper" and there is strong suspicion from some of the investigators that the letters were actually from journalists attempting to keep the "story" of Jack the Ripper going.

The name of "Jack the Ripper" wasn't used in the early cases and didn't become commonplace until the letters appeared after the double event. The use of the name "Jack" was common for criminals and like many of the letters, it was believed to be journalists who started utilizing the name of "Jack the Ripper". Prior to that, he was known as the Whitechapel Murderer or often, Leather Apron.

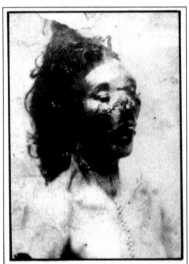

Catherine Eddowes
victim #4

(above) A sketch of Mitre Square with the body of Catherine Eddowes in the position she was found (at the front center of the sketch).

(Left) The mortuary picture of Catherine Eddowes.

(bottom) An illustration sketch drawn to show the position of Eddowes' body when it was found.

FIVE WEEKS HAD PASSED SINCE THE DOUBLE EVENT. HAD THE RIPPER *DISAPPEARED?*...

IN *MILLER'S COURT,* A FIRE RAGED SO HOT, IT *MELTED* SOME OF THE UTENSILS.

AND IT PROVIDED LIGHT FOR THE MOST HORRIFIC MURDER YET, THAT OF *MARY JANE KELLY.*

THE DOOR, *LOCKED* FROM WITHIN, HELD THIS GRIZZLY MURDER FROM VIEW ON THE BUSY STREET OUTSIDE. IT WAS THE *ONLY* MURDER KNOWN TO OCCUR *INDOORS.*

WAS THIS TRULY THE *LAST* OF THE RIPPER'S VICTIMS? WAS "JACK" SEARCHING FOR THIS ONE *FINAL* TESTAMENT TO HIS BIZARRE AGENDA?

OR WAS SOMETHING MORE *SINISTER* INVOLVED...SOMETHING THAT WASN'T TOTALLY *RANDOM?*

WHATEVER THE CASE, ON NOVEMBER 9, 1888, MARY KELLY DIED. THE *SAVAGERY* OF HER DEATH STUNNED EVEN THE MOST *HARDENED* INVESTIGATORS.

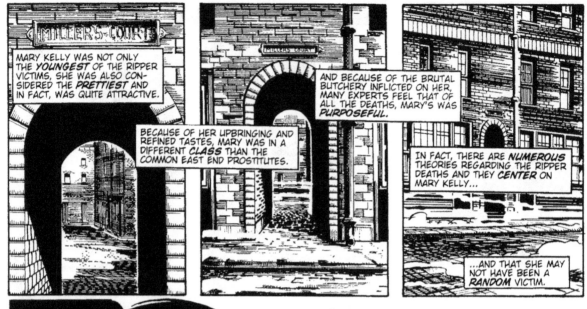

MARY KELLY WAS NOT ONLY THE *YOUNGEST* OF THE RIPPER VICTIMS, SHE WAS ALSO CONSIDERED THE *PRETTIEST* AND IN FACT, WAS QUITE ATTRACTIVE.

BECAUSE OF HER UPBRINGING AND REFINED TASTES, MARY WAS IN A DIFFERENT *CLASS* THAN THE COMMON EAST END PROSTITUTES.

AND BECAUSE OF THE BRUTAL BUTCHERY INFLICTED ON HER, MANY EXPERTS FEEL THAT OF ALL THE DEATHS, MARY'S WAS *PURPOSEFUL.*

IN FACT, THERE ARE *NUMEROUS* THEORIES REGARDING THE RIPPER DEATHS AND THEY *CENTER* ON MARY KELLY...

...AND THAT SHE MAY NOT HAVE BEEN A *RANDOM* VICTIM.

ONE OF THE MOST *POPULAR* THEORIES REGARDING THE RIPPER MURDERS WAS INTRODUCED BY STEPHEN KNIGHT AND HAS SINCE SPAWNED NUMEROUS BOOKS AND MOVIES AND, TO MANY PEOPLE, HAS NOW PROVEN THE ANSWER TO THE LONG DEBATED QUESTION OF WHO THE RIPPER WAS. IT HAS BEEN MODIFIED BY SOME, BUT ESSENTIALLY, THIS THEORY BEGINS WITH THE DUKE OF CLARENCE MARRYING A YOUNG CATHOLIC GIRL NAMED ALICE ELIZABETH CROOK. OF COURSE, THERE WAS AN UPROAR AT THE ROYAL HOUSE BECAUSE OF CROOK BEING CATHOLIC. THE MARRIAGE WAS TO BE DISSOLVED WITH NO RECORD OF IT, HOWEVER, *TWO* PROBLEMS HAD OCCURRED. THE FIRST WAS THAT A CHILD HAD BEEN BORN. THE SECOND WAS THAT A WOMAN HAD WITNESSED THE WEDDING AND KNEW ALICE CROOK QUITE WELL.

HER NAME WAS *MARY KELLY.*

CROOK AND HER DAUGHTER WERE ABDUCTED BY THE GOVERNMENT. OF THE DAUGHTER NOTHING IS KNOWN, BUT CROOK, SUPPOSEDLY UNDERGOING SOME SURGERY TO DISTORT HER MEMORY, DIED EARLY IN WORKING HOUSES. HOWEVER MARY KELLY, THE WITNESS, HAD PLANS TO PROTECT HERSELF. FALLING INTO PROSTITUTION, SHE ENLISTED THREE OF HER FRIENDS TO HELP BLACKMAIL THE AUTHORITIES. HER FRIENDS WERE POLLY NICHOLS, ANNE CHAPMAN, AND ELIZABETH STRIDE. SIR WILLIAM GULL, PHYSICIAN TO THE COURT WAS PUT IN CHARGE OF *SILENCING* THE BLACKMAILERS, AND HE, ALONG WITH TWO OTHERS, JOHN NEDLEY AND WILLIAM SICKERT BEGAN TO KILL THE WOMEN AND MAKE THE MURDERS LOOK LIKE THE WORK OF A *MADMAN.*

CATHERINE EDDOWES WAS NOT AN INTENDED VICTIM, BUT BECAUSE OF THE CONFUSION AT THE POLICE STATION WITH THE NAME KELLY, SHE WAS ACCIDENTALLY MURDERED. THE REAL KELLY (*MARY*) WOULD MEET HER FATE SOME FIVE WEEKS LATER.

SINCE THE RELEASE OF THE BOOK BY KNIGHT, ONE OF THE PRIMARY SOURCES, JOSEPH SICKERT, DESCENDANT OF WILLIAM, SAID THAT THE WHOLE STORY WAS MADE UP...A *HOAX.* MANY RIPPEROLOGISTS DO NOT BELIEVE THIS VERSION HAS ANY MERIT, BUT IT STILL REMAINS A FASCINATING AND INGENIOUS TALE.

THE · PENNY
ILLUSTRATED · PAPER
AND · ILLUSTRATED TIMES

No. 1453.—Vol. 55.   November 17, 1888

REGISTERED AT THE GENERAL POST-OFFICE AS A NEWSPAPER.

London : Printed and Published at the Office, 10, Milford-lane, Strand, in the Parish of St. Clement Danes, in the County of Middlesex, by Thomas Fox, 10, Milford-lane, Strand, aforesaid.

MILLER'S COURT

ENTRANCE TO MILLER'S COURT IN DORSET STREET

IT WAS THROUGH THE BROKEN PANES OF THIS WINDOW THAT THE BODY OF THE MURDERED WOMAN WAS FIRST SEEN

THE MILLER-COURT MURDER, WHITECHAPEL: SITE OF MARY KELLY'S LODGINGS.

VICTIM #5 — MARY KELLY

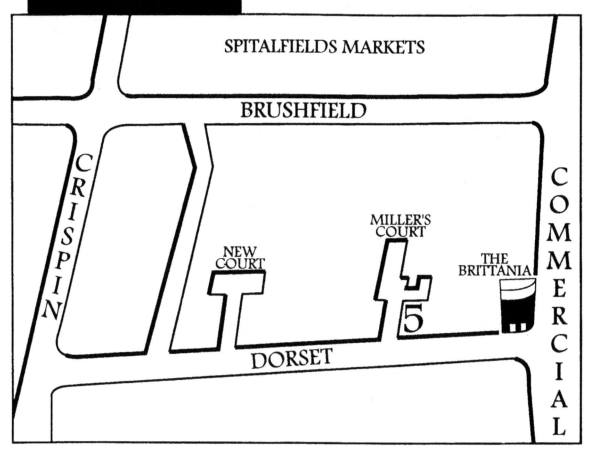

MILLER'S COURT · NOVEMBER 9, 1888

Miller's Court. That was the location of where Mary Kelly had perished and it remains as one of the examples of sheer brutality in the annals of crime. Even though Jack the Ripper at the time was being labeled as the murderer of up to seven woman, it was this final murder that permanently installed him as the demonic master of horror.

Mary Kelly was last seen entering her home with a "client" around midnight and witnesses also mentioned that Mary could be heard singing around 1:00 a.m. Whether her client had departed by then, it is unsure. It wasn't until nearly 11:00 that morning that someone went to find Mary and her body was discovered.·

It was uncertain how Mary descended into prostitution. She was born in Limerick and her family moved to Wales where her father was a foreman at an ironworks. Mary seemed to have a good life and married at age 16. Her husband was killed a couple of years later in an explosion and at age 21, with little to leave, Mary departed for London. Almost immediately, she took on work at a brothel in the upper class section of the West End. She linked herself to a few clients and one even took her to France. She alternated between prostitution and serving as a companion for others before she settled in the East End. She had a long relationship with a plasterer before she met Joe Barnett who she ended up living with for the last year of her life. The biggest question with most Ripperologists would be why would Mary with so many advantages and good looks descend so rapidly into prostitution? Even while she was living with Barnett, she still engaged in prostitution at their home of 13 Miller's Court when money was tight, which obviously did not sit well with Barnett. After a fight, Barnett left Miller's Court a few days before the murder. Naturally, he was the prime suspect at first but later was declared innocent.

When Thomas Bowyer knocked on Mary's door that morning in an attempt to collect rent, he received no answer. Since the door was locked from the inside, he assumed that she was still inside and so going around to the window, he peeked inside to see if perhaps he could wake her from the deep sleep she must have fallen into. The sight immediately sent him off to the police.

MARY KELLY

Report from *THE ILLUSTRATED POLICE NEWS:*

"The throat had been cut right across with a knife, nearly severing the head from the body. The abdomen had been partially ripped open, and both of the breasts had been cut from the body, the left arm, like the head, hung to body by the skin only. The nose had been cut off, the forehead skinned, and the thighs, down to the feet, stripped of the flesh. The abdomen had been slashed with a knife across downwards, and the liver and entrails wrenched away. The entrails and other portions of the frame were missing, but the liver, it is said, was found placed between the feet of this poor victim. The flesh from the thighs and legs, together with the breasts and nose, had been placed by the murderer on the table, and one of the hands of the dead woman had been pushed into her stomach."

It was later reported that Mary Kelly was three months pregnant and that her heart was taken from the scene by the murderer.

Mary Kelly is considered the last of the Ripper murders. Today, as back then, there was a great deal of disagreement among the investigators

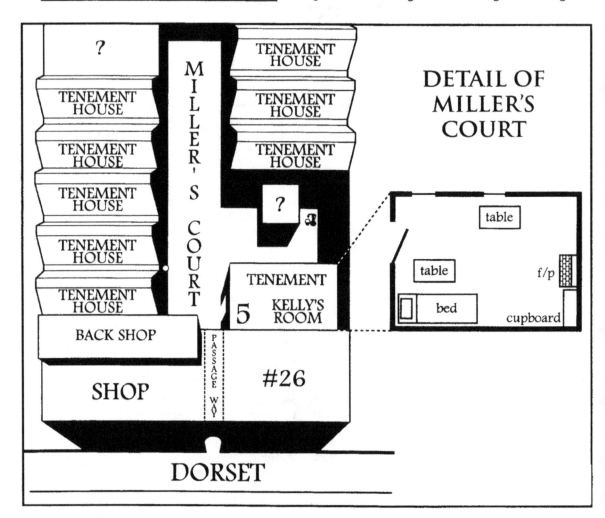

DETAIL OF MILLER'S COURT

Although Mary Kelly had died broke and in prostitution at the age of 25, her funeral would give an indication of wealth and fame as she was attended by a funeral hearse with two mourning coaches and 100's of people following behind. At the Church service, there were several thousand people who came to pay their respects to the latest unfortunate victim of Jack the Ripper.

An illustration showing Mary Jane Kelly also known as Black Mary or Marie Jeanette Kelly, standing outside of her room at Miller's Court. (right) Sketch showing a photographer taking pictures of Kelly's ravaged body as she lay on her bed.

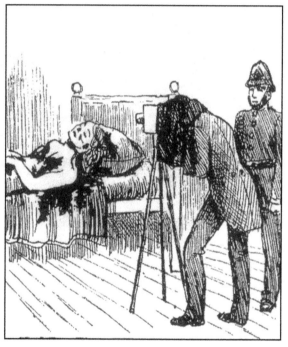

A picture of the outside of Kelly's room at Miller's Court. The room was small but typical, measuring about 12 feet square.

Surprisingly, shortly after Mary Kelly's death, interest in the Ripper murders from the press and newspapers died down. After months of being the main topic in London, there were only short bursts of interest that quickly waned. Any murder of women in Whitechapel would renew the fears and speculation but the few that occurred were quickly dismissed. As the year ended, it seemed as though Jack the Ripper had ended his crusade...but still kept his identity a secret.

The following are some of the more well known suspects who are often associated with being Jack the Ripper. Some have valid points to consider whereas others can be dismissed rather quickly. It is worth mentioning them here, even if it is just to eliminate them from contention. There is a great deal of additional information available on most of these suspects and most have one or more books dedicated to the theories.

In dealing with the possible suspects, there are a few informational sources that need to be referred to as they provide a great deal of information and cast suspicion on some of the suspects.

The Macnaughton Memoranda

This was written by Sir Melville Macnaughton who joined the CID, less than a year after the Ripper murders. Although he did not participate in the investigation, he was in charge of assimilating much of the information as he was promoted to Chief Constable and later, Assistant Commissioner.

Macnaughton issued a response in 1894 to a newspaper article that claimed the Ripper had been discovered, A Thomas Cutbush. After discussing the ill merits of Cutbush as a suspect, Macnaughton listed five victims and five victims only (and these are those who are considered by most as the Ripper victims). He also listed the three primary suspects and these were Druitt, Kominski, and Ostrog.

The Royal Conspiracy

Through a series of books and theories, many members of the Royal Family were pulled into the Ripper research. Names such as Stephens, Gull, Duke of Clarence, and others were integral to many of the different theories proposed with most centering around the Duke of Clarence, heir to the throne of England.

Joseph Barnett

Barnett was the live in companion with Mary Kelly, the last of the Ripper victims. There is a considerable amount of links to Kelly, obviously. Although Barnett was questioned initially, that would be a natural part of the investigation. It wasn't until the 1970's that Barnett's name surfaced as a suspect.

Applying the techniques of the FBI serial killer profiling, Barnett fit the type in a psychological match which although an aid to the FBI, certainly does not indicate homicidal tendencies.

The logic of Barnett's case was that he was tired of Mary relying on prostitution to earn money and disgusted with himself for being unable to provide for her. In order to keep her off the streets, he began to murder prostitutes to scare her off. When she didn't and he realized that she would never love him the way he loved her, he killed and mutilated her body in a jealous rage.

The case for Barnett is rather weak. Many of the different aspects fit nearly in but seem in contrast with the person. It appears to be a carefully constructed case of what if and making sure everything fits into place. Unfortunately for the memory of Joseph Barnett, it does...whether he was the murderer or not.

George Chapman- See Severin Klosowski.

Dr. Thomas Neill Cream

Cream is a notorious figure in crime lore. A doctor of honors who entered the field of abortion. He was also involved in numerous murders in Canada, the United States, and England. Utilizing poison as his weapon, there is very little to connect him to the Ripper murders.

Except one thing.

As Cream was having the noose tightened around his neck, he bellowed out the following words before the bottom dropped out. " I am Jack..."

And thus, Cream is part of the Ripper lore.

However, he is virtually and almost instantly discredited because he was serving jail time in America during the Ripper murders. He is mentioned here solely to eliminate any confusion to the validity of his being Jack the Ripper.

Montague John Druitt

Frederick Bailey Deeming

Deeming was sentenced to death for the murder of his wife. This was his second wife and it was discovered that he also murdered his first wife and their four children.

While in prison awaiting execution, Deeming confessed that he was Jack the Ripper. Although the police did not take his claims seriously as Deeming was in prison at the time of the murders, the press had no such reluctance. They gave credence to his claim.

A death mask was formed from Deeming's face and for years, it was immortalized as the face of Jack the Ripper. The mask now resides in the infamous Black Museum and Deeming is no longer considered a serious candidate for Jack the Ripper, even by the press.

Montague John Druitt

For over 70 years, Ripperologists had discussed one of the prime suspects yet did not know his name. All that was known of this likely suspect was that he was a man who had committed suicide right after the last Ripper murder. It seemed to fit into the police view as well, as for most, the investigation into the Ripper murders also ceased.

In what is known as the Macnaughton Memoranda, Sir Melville listed Druitt by name but the report was not uncovered again until 1959. Ripperologists at first, believed that they finally had an answer to the perplexing question of who Jack

Sir William Gull

the Ripper was. Druitt fit the profile in many ways. He was a doctor in good social standing and Macnaughton had reason to feel that Druitt was likely the Ripper.

As the case regarding Druitt began to be investigated by researchers, it became readily apparent that nothing linked Druitt to the crimes.

Although there was some strong evidence that Druitt did not commit the crimes, it wasn't conclusive enough to eliminate him as a suspect. One of the key elements was the timing of Druitt's suicide which was right after the last murder. The whole matter then came down to the suspicions by Mcnaughton.

Macnaughton said that Druitt was a doctor, however he was actually a barrister who taught school. There are no reasons for his suicide that are evident except perhaps Druitt's belief that he would go insane like his mother. There is a question concerning his termination from his teaching job. Some feel there was a hint of a homosexual incident that caused his dismissal. However, judging from family history, it was apparent that suicidal tendencies ran in Druitt's family (his mother had attempted it. His grandmother and sister were successful in their attempts)

The major reason (and only thus far) that Druitt is under suspicion is because of Macnaughton's assertion. Either Macnaughton based his information on something that has yet to be uncovered, or else he was mis-informed.

Sir William Gull

Gull, the physician of the Royal family, is the centerpiece of this elaborate theory. It was formed from the controversial book, Jack the Ripper: The Final Solution by Stephen Knight. It was also popularized in the film, "Murder by Decree" as well as the excellent comic series, "From Hell". Both are highly entertaining works that should be enjoyed on their own merits and not whether they are indeed, the final solution.

The basic premise is that Eddy struck up a relationship with a young girl, Annie Crook, who was a Catholic. She became pregnant so Eddy arranged a secret marriage. Of course, this could not be condoned, and Eddy was pulled back into the safety of the palace and Annie Crook was sent to one of Gull's hospitals. Annie had a friend who helped to watch the child. The friend was Mary Kelly.

Kelly realized the potential for disaster and decided that by blackmailing the Crown, she could end her life of misery. She confided in the scheme with some of her friends, (Chapman, Nicols, and Stride) and sent word that they could be bought off.

Gull was brought in again to eliminate the problem. Using John Netley, a coachman, Gull created a murderer from his belief in Masonic rituals. Even some of the police were Masons, and therefore, forced to go along with the scheme. Gull and Netley carried out the murders as they found the women. Eddowes was a mistake (for she had given her name as Mary Kelly at the police station). After the murder of the real Mary Kelly, the murders stopped. The police utilized the suicide of Druitt to come up with a potential scapegoat.

The theory has been resoundly attacked by many Ripperologists but it continues as the most popular and has now cemented itself as a part of history to many people.

Jill the Ripper

This theory states that only a woman could have successfully committed the murders and got away with it. There are no clues pointing to any specific woman but rather in lieu of having evidence against a man committing the crime, it therefore, must have a been a woman.

Only a woman would have the opportunity to blend in with the crowd and escape notice, especially if the woman were a mid-wife. A mid-wife walking the streets with blood stained clothes

Jill the Ripper

would draw no attention to herself. At that time, a woman carrying out such brutal crimes would hardly even be considered.

The imperial evidence supporting this theory is nil. It exists simply as a way of attempting to find an answer to an unanswerable crime.

Severin Klosowski

Also known as *George Chapman*. He was a Polish assistant surgeon who came to London in February of 1887 and became a hairdresser. He married and had a son that died soon after birth. In 1891, he and his wife moved to New York. Less than two years later they returned to London but not together. His wife had come back to London after Klosowski had attacked her with a knife. He followed but the relationship was over. Klosowski continued his work as a hairdresser and met another woman (oddly enough, named Annie Chapman...the same name as one of the Ripper's victims!). After that relationship dissolved, Severin Klosowski was no more and he became known as George Chapman.

In 1895, Chapman married again but it was unofficial. Although the marriage was not legal, the couple operated a barber shop together and things seemed to be going well. However, soon his wife became ill and died. Over the next six years, Chapman would marry twice more in illegal marriages and again, his wives died. There were numerous reports that he also beat his wives.

After the death of the third wife, police exhumed the bodies of his first two wives. They had been poisoned with arsenic and antimony which helped to preserve the bodies. Chapman was tried and convicted. He was hung in April of 1903.

Chapman became a suspect during the investigation of his wife murders. One of the inspectors started investigating the case and realized that not only did Chapman have the necessary surgical skills to perform the Ripper's cuttings, but his personality also lent itself to a profile of the Ripper. Inspector Abberline, on an independent investigation, also came up to the same conclusion. George Chapman was Jack the Ripper.

The circumstantial evidence was there. Chapman was in London at the time of the murders and had opportunities that weren't eliminated by any alibis. In fact, during the time that Chapman was in New York, there were some similar murders there and of course, the murders stopped in London. Abberline's investigation revealed that an American had contacted many doctors in London seeking internal organs. This quickly led to the conclusion that Jack...or Chapman had mutilated the bodies in order to obtain the organs. Perhaps Chapman's excursion to New York was to be closer to the buyer of the organs taken from victims.

The major problem of Chapman is the change in methods. Most modern profilers feel that someone that enacted his rage like knifings would not switch to poison, especially in the case of Jack the Ripper who seemingly was intensifying his mutilations with each succeeding victim. Another

Severin Klosowski

problem is that Chapman was not known to speak English clearly and with the witnesses reports, there was never any mention of any of the potential suspects limited by the lack of English.

So, Chapman or Klosowski is indeed an intriguing suspect, one that cannot be easily eliminated. That however, does not automatically mean he is Jack the Ripper. But many believe, his is the most solid case.

Aaron Kominsky

A strong candidate for the Ripper and one that many Ripperologists will come to agreement on. Even though there are some concerns. Mentioned in the Macnaughton Memoranda and referred to by Sir Robert Anderson who was Assistant Commissioner of the Metropolitan Police. Anderson stated that the identity of Jack the Ripper was known and all of his correspondence leads to Kominsky. Anderson claimed that a witness positively identified the Ripper and other papers identified Kominsky as a violent man which tied into the Macnaughton description "...had a great hatred of women, specially of the prostitute class, and had strong homicidal tendencies: he was removed to a lunatic asylum about March 1889. "

Kominsky fit the bill in many cases. However, researchers are unable to find who would be the credible witness that could have identify Kominsky. Although Kominsky was indeed put away in an insane asylum, reports of his behavior did not indicate the violent nature the police had reported. Perhaps the major problem with Kominsky is that a period of two years had passed from the last murder (Mary Kelly) before he was incarcerated in the asylum. Obviously, someone of the deranged nature of Jack the Ripper, would not have ceased killing based on scientific reports of the nature of killers such as Jack.

The Lodger

Not a specified person but a madman who had escaped from an asylum and carried out a religious vendetta against the whores of the world and would find a way to cleanse the spoiled environs of the East End. Built upon the claims of Dr. L. Forbes Winslow, the theory quickly fell apart. However, the long lasting image of the mysterious lodger was immortalized by the work of Mrs. Belloc Lowndes's fictional character.

James Maybrick

Revealed as the Ripper in the long lost diary, poor James Maybrick fortunately only had to suffer the indignity of being a Ripper suspect for a few years before the diary was revealed to be a total fraud.

Michael Ostrog

According to the official Scotland Yard reports, Michael Ostrog was a Russian doctor and a convict who was subsequently detained in a lunatic asylum as a homicidal maniac. His whereabouts at the time of the murders (Jack the Ripper's) could never be ascertained. Macnaugton also named Ostrog as one of the three leading candidates for the Ripper.

Ostrog was a man of relatively good background and a proper home life. He spend the years of 1866 to 1887 in and out of jail, mostly for crimes of theft. He had served time in an asylum which gave credence to his mental state.

When the police were searching for suspects for the Ripper, it was obvious that criminals were looked at and here is where Ostrog's name came up. He was considered a viable suspect because of his background. When the Macnaughton Memoranda listed his name and a description of his behavior, again it was another exciting candidate.

However, further research also invalidates Ostrog as the Ripper murderer. From the few witnesses who testified and may have seen the Ripper, none match Ostrog's description. Also, contrary to the disposition of Ostrog stated by police in their subsequent reports, Ostrog was more of a con artist than a violent character and his one episode of "mental illness" may actually have been a ruse by him to avoid heading to prison again. The claim of Ostrog carrying surgical knives around (which would lead one to suspect foul play) can be explained easily enough by the fact that Ostrog often impersonated being a doctor to carry out his con games and the medical bag with surgical instruments was a necessary prop.

Dr. Pedachenko

This character is in the middle of a confusing muddle of the Ripper murders that connects with the George Chapman / Severin Klosowski consideration. It is said by some that Pedachenko committed the crimes. The reason, to embarrass the British as Pedachenko was sent by the Russian Bolsheviks to prove immortality of the Capitalistic system. There are others that claim that Pedachenko, who had an uncanny resemblance to Klosowski was actually Klosowski using yet another alias.

Duke of Clarence

Prince Albert Victor Christian Edward "Eddy"

The Duke of Clarence is one of the most famous names in Ripper lore. He is the centerpiece to at least three of the center Ripper theories. Eddy was considered a slow child, perhaps even suffering from a mild form of retardation. The theory that is directly linked to Eddy is that he went mad from syphilis and thus, took revenge on the prostitutes that gave him the deadly disease. The Royal family quickly found out about Eddy's participation and locked him away after the double murder. However, Eddy escaped and committed the final and horrendous crime on Mary Kelly. Afterwards, Eddy was recaptured and taken to an insane asylum where he died in 1892. His cause of death was officially listed as dying from influenza.

Eddy's role as Jack the Ripper has not survived with most of the experts investigating the murders although he has a stronger validation as being the principle in other theories. After his supposed incarceration in the insane asylum, Eddy made

James K. Stephen

frequent public appearance. And the most telling evidence of all is that Eddy could be accounted for, often outside of the country, during the murders.

James K. Stephen

James Stephen was Eddy's tutor at Cambridge and during their time together, a sexual relationship formed. After Eddy left, Stephen continued his career until a head accident drove him to madness. Stephen decides to avenge himself upon Eddy in a bizarre blood rite that ties in with Greek and Roman mythology.

Although Stephen was an intriguing character and Eddy continues to pop up in different theories, this is probably the weakest theory involving the Duke of Calrence. There is no evidence that supports Stephen's role in committing the murders.

Dr. Stanley

This was a mysterious figure known only as Dr. Stanley who apparently confessed that he was jack the Ripper. The motive for his murders was to avenge his son who had died of venereal disease contacted two years prior by a Mary Kelly.

Stanley wanted revenge and he set out to

get it. In order to hide his crime, he had to kill other prostitutes to deflect attention for his primary target, Mary Kelly. This logic also explains why Kelly was so brutally mutilated as she was the cause of his son's death. He then fled to South America.

There is not a great amount of plausible evidence supporting this theory. There isn't a concrete trail of a Dr. Stanley that matches the events that transpired, although it certainly could have been an assumed name. Furthermore, syphilis does not kill within two years as Stanley (a supposed doctor) had claimed. Mary Kelly was not listed as having venereal disease but it may not have been looked for in light of the condition of her body at death.

The Dr. Stanley theory has little going for it as there is no substantial information that accompanies the theory.

Francis Tumblety

Tumblety was a doctor who left the United States after, as he claimed, he was being falsely accused of participating in the Lincoln Assassination. After touring Europe and returning periodically to the United States, Tumblety's name surfaces as he was arrested in 1888 for homosexual activities. He was then charged for suspicion in the Whitechapel murders. There is no strong evidence that supports the claim of the inspector who felt Tumblety was the killer and what led the inspector to suspect Tumblety.

However, Tumblety had escaped to America where he managed to hide out. Scotland Yard definitely seemed interested and it is believed they sent one of their own after him. Tumblety was never apprehended and died in 1903.

It is suspected by some that although Tumblety's name is a fairly recent one, there is a great amount of support even though there is not chain of evidence against him. A lot of the other criteria fits in. As for the quietness of Scotland Yard, it may be perhaps because they let their number one suspect get away. Announcing the identity of Jack the Ripper but unable to apprehend him would be worse than not identifying him at all.

The case of Tumblety as Jack the Ripper needs further research to see if he should, indeed, be considered a prime suspect.

????

The answer to was actually Jack the Ripper may never be known. Some feel that it has to be somebody important, thus accounting for the inconclusiveness of the police investigating the crimes. Perhaps that's why the Royal Conspiracy theories are so popular.

But for most, the answer is part of the intriguing aspect of Jack the Ripper. If the case ever becomes solved, will it lose the fascination which bind so many of us to it in a perverse manner.

Who knows? That is what compels us so much...because we don't know the answer.

References

There are a number of non-fiction books about Jack the Ripper and they are usually broken down into two areas. One will be sifting through all the available information and reconstructing the investigation and suspect list and the other side will be bringing up obscure references and building a case against a particular suspect. I don't mean to suggest that these approaches should be viewed in a derogatory way...not at all. Any information that does come forward regarding Jack is often from the investigative and creative thinking that many of these writers put into their theories. At the very least, the process does eliminate quite a few suspects.

Being an avid reader of material on Jack the Ripper, I also consulted a number of books. Many are similar but these are the ones I found to be most useful. Since the time of the writing of this comic/book, there have been a number of new and exciting voyages into the world of The Ripper but they are not listed here as they were not references I used at the time.

The Complete History of Jack the Ripper. *Philip Sugden*, Carroll & Graf. 1994.

Jack the Ripper: The Complete Casebook. *Donald Rumbelow*, Contemporary Books, 1988.

The Diary of Jack the Ripper. Smith & Gryphon. Oct. 1993.

The Jack the Ripper A to Z. *Begg, Paul, Martin Fido & Keith Skinner*, Headline Book Publishing, 1991.

Jack the Ripper: The Final Solution. *Stephen Knight*, George G. Harrap & Co Ltd, 1976

Jack the Ripper: The Simple Truth. *Bruce Paley*. Headline Book Publishing, 1995.

CREATORS

Gary Reed has written a number of graphic novels including A Killing of Scarecrows, Renfield. Deadworld, Baker Street, Saint Germaine, Red Diaries and many more. He often worked with historical or literary settings and some of his books have been used in college classrooms for both literature and as comic writing guides. He is probably best known for his long running series, Deadworld, which received numerous awards and nominations over the last ten years. He was also the publisher of Caliber Comics which help launch the careers of many of the top talents in the comic industry today. When he was not involved in storytelling, Gary was an Adjunct Professor of Biology at community colleges in the Detroit/Ann Arbor area until his passing in 2016. He is survived by his wife, Jennifer, and four daughters.

MARK BLOODWORTH is a storyteller and artist who created the critically favored, urban crime comic book: Nightstreets for Arrow Comics. This led to him being contracted by Marvel Comics to create character design, spot illos, and story art for Clive Barker's: Hellraiser. He has illustrated a number of comics including Cheerleaders from Hell, Jack the Ripper, Raven Chronicles, Deadworld, The Ripper Legacy, Negative Burn and the critically hailed Abel, written by William Harms. He is currently working on a number of various projects but prefers to announce them only when ready to appear. Mark is also working with film director, Douglas Schulze on his latest movie endeavor providing storyboards, concept and production art.

Art Credits

Mark Bloodworth
pages 2, 12-15, 17, 19, 20, 22, 23, 25, 26, 28, 29, 33-36, 39, 40, 43, 44, 47-51

Gustave Dore
pages 5-10, 46

Contemporary newspapers and illustrations
pages 11, 16, 18, 21, 24, 27, 30-32, 37, 38, 41, 42, 45

ALSO AVAILABLE FROM CALIBER COMICS

QUALITY GRAPHIC NOVELS TO ENTERTAIN

THE SEARCHERS: VOLUME 1
The Shape of Things to Come

Before League of Extraordinary Gentlemen there was The Searchers. At the dawn of the 20th century the greatest literary adventurers from the likes of Wells, Verne, Doyle, Burroughs, and Haggard were created. All thought to be the work of pure fiction. However, a century later, the real-life descendants of those famous adventurers are recruited by the legendary Professor Challenger in order to save mankind's future. Collected for the first time.

"Searchers is the comic book I have on the wall with a sign reading - 'Love books? Never read a comic? Try this one! ....money back guarantee..." - Dark Star Books.

WAR OF THE WORLDS: INFESTATION

Based on the H.G. Wells classic! The "Martian Invasion" has begun again and now mankind must fight for its very humanity. It happened slowly at first but by the third year, it seemed that the war was almost over... the war was almost lost.

"Writer Randy Zimmerman has a fine grasp of drama, and spins the various strands of the story into a coherent whole... imaginative and very gritty."
- war-of-the-worlds.co.uk

HELSING: LEGACY BORN

From writer Gary Reed (Deadworld) and artists John Lowe (Captain America), Bruce McCorkindale (Godzilla). She was born into a legacy she wanted no part of and pushed into a battle recessed deep in the shadows of the night. Samantha Helsing is torn between two worlds...two allegiances...two families. The legacy of the Van Helsing family and their crusade against the "night creatures" comes to modern day with the most unlikely of all warriors.

"Congratulations on this masterpiece..."
- Paul Dale Roberts, Compuserve Reviews

"All in all, another great package from Caliber."
- Paul Haywood, Comics Forum

DEADWORLD

Before there was The Walking Dead there was Deadworld. Here is an introduction of the long running classic horror series, Deadworld, to a new audience! Considered by many to be the godfather of the original zombie comic with over 100 issues and graphic novels in print and over 1,000,000 copies sold, Deadworld ripped into the undead with intelligent zombies on a mission and a group of poor teens riding in a school bus desperately try to stay one step ahead of the sadistic, Harley-riding King Zombie. Death, mayhem, and a touch of supernatural evil made Deadworld a classic and now here's your chance to get into the story!

DAYS OF WRATH

Award winning comic writer & artist Wayne Vansant brings his gripping World War II saga of war in the Pacific to Guadalcanal and the Battle of Bloody Ridge. This is the powerful story of the long, vicious battle for Guadalcanal that occurred in 1942-43. When the U.S. Navy orders its outnumbered and outgunned ships to run from the Japanese fleet, they abandon American troops on a bloody, battered island in the South Pacific.

"Heavy on authenticity, compellingly written and beautifully drawn."
- Comics Buyers Guide

BECK and CAUL INVESTIGATIONS:
Where the Nightmares Walk
- Collects the entire Beck & Caul series for the FIRST TIME!

There is a place where evil lives. Where all of mankind's nightmares are a reality. It is the Underside. From this realm of myth and shadow was born Jonas Beck who teams up with a young woman, Mercedes Guillane and their paths meld into one...to battle evil in all its guises. Set in the voodoo influenced city of New Orleans, Beck and Caul are paranormal detectives who scrounge the streets of this dark, mystical city in order to combat and protect people from supernatural attacks and events.

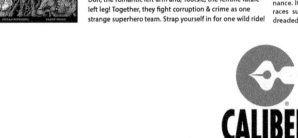

COUNTER-PARTS

From best selling author Stefan Petrucha (MARVEL's Deadpool, Captain America). Think people can be disingenuous? Of course and in the future they try on new personas like hats. But when Hieronymus Jones overdoses on TPGs (temporary personality grafts), his original personality is destroyed. Now an experimental cure gives him not 1, but 6 new personalities. Each inhabiting a different part of his body. There's: Bogey, the hard-boiled right arm; Kik-li, the Kung-Fu master right leg; Jake, the self-involved torso; Buckley, the too-smart head; Don, the romantic left arm and; Tootsie, the femme fatale left leg! Together, they fight corruption & crime as one strange superhero team. Strap yourself in for one wild ride!

LEGENDLORE

From Caliber Comics now comes the entire Realm and Legendlore saga as a set of volumes that collects the long running critically acclaimed series. In the vein of The Lord of The Rings and The Hobbit with elements of Game of Thrones and Dungeon and Dragons.

Four normal modern day teenagers are plunged into a world they thought only existed in novels and film. They are whisked away to a magical land where dragons roam the skies, orcs and hobgoblins terrorize travelers, where unicorns prance through the forest, and kingdoms wage war for dominance. It is a world where man is just one race, joining other races such as elves, trolls, dwarves, changelings, and the dreaded night creatures who steal the night.

CALIBER
COMICS

www.calibercomics.com